The Mind's Empty Tomb

The Mind's Empty Tomb

Reflections on Mental Illness through the Easter Story

David B. Morgan

RESOURCE *Publications* • Eugene, Oregon

THE MIND'S EMPTY TOMB
Reflections on Mental Illness through the Easter Story

Resource Publications
An Imprint of Wipf and Stock Publishers
199 W. 8th Ave., Suite 3
Eugene, OR 97401

www.wipfandstock.com

PAPERBACK ISBN: 978-1-6667-8421-3
HARDCOVER ISBN: 978-1-6667-8422-0
EBOOK ISBN: 978-1-6667-8423-7

VERSION NUMBER 08/31/23

Contents

Introduction

E XPERIENCING MENTAL ILLNESS—WHETHER SUFFERING from it yourself, or watching someone you love suffer—can be a dark and confusing experience. I know that firsthand.

During a particularly acute bout of mental illness, and then the subsequent recovery phase, I was struck by the possible relationship between this experience and the dark and confusing experience of living through Jesus' passion and resurrection. I'm certainly not suggesting that suffering mental ill health is to experience one's own crucifixion, or that suffering in this way is somehow redemptive. Suffering is a very real aspect of our present reality, but I don't think that 'God gives us suffering' as some kind of character formation. Nor do I think that the crucifixion of Christ is a metaphor for mental illness. It simply seems to me that the general pattern of such a well-known story, and the central event of Christianity, might be a way of beginning to understand one story of mental illness.

Neither will this slim volume tell you how to 'fix' a mental health problem. I am not a doctor, but I believe that many things which are labelled as mental illness can't be 'fixed'. My own experience is that it is more about learning to live with them, with the help of some of the various means of support available. I am certainly not 'fixed'. I would not even say that I have fully recovered. I am obviously much better than I was at my worst, though I still rely heavily on medication. The bad days are not frequent, but they come around often enough to remind me that mental illness is something with which I am still living, and with which I will probably always be living. I believe fervently in the power of prayer, and in the possibility of miraculous God-given healing. If you want to be 'fixed', I would certainly not stop you praying for that. But I don't think it is something which we can achieve by our own efforts; and even if it is, you won't find much help towards that goal here.

What you will find are my own personal reflections on my own personal experiences, mediated through a selection of lenses in the passion narratives. There are autobiographical elements, and reflections of a theological nature, along with some of my own thoughts on the topic of mental health. Akin to the traditional 'stations of the cross', we enter the Biblical story for a dozen small moments, rather than taking in a grand sweep of events. I am no expert in mental health issues, and I am no more qualified than the average priest as a Biblical scholar; this is in no way an academic work, either of psychology or theology. My experience is certainly not all-embracing, and nor would I claim it as normative. But it is mine, I don't think it is unique, and I offer it in the hope that it may just help somebody else.

Betrayed

When it was evening, he took his place with the twelve;
and while they were eating, he said, "Truly I tell you, one
of you will betray me."—Matt 26:20–21

I WAS TWENTY-THREE WHEN I was first diagnosed with depression, although with the benefit of hindsight I realized that I had been living with its shadow for longer. Like many people, it had begun for me earlier in adolescence. Its effects put strain on friendships, affected relationships, cost professional and educational opportunities. At times I ate far too much, or far too little. Sometimes I drank more alcohol than was probably sensible, and certainly more than was ideal. It disrupted my sleeping patterns, so that I veered between insomnia and lethargy. But those are the outward signs of mental illness. The inner experience is different, and in many ways more disturbing.

My experience of the outward signs is that I did not like or enjoy them, even while they were happening. It wasn't a conscious decision on my part to be staying awake late into the night, for example, or conversely to be craving sixteen hours or more sleep every day. In fact, both of those things were unwelcome, and often proved to be inconvenient at best and destructive at worst. I knew when I was drinking too much, or eating too much. I wasn't doing these things because I particularly wanted to. Sometimes I actively did not want to, but ended up doing them anyway. They were almost compulsive habits. When I was in the grip of illness, I simply couldn't help myself, or stop myself.

My experience of mental illness has been that, when I am feeling ill, I become almost a bystander in my own life. I will find myself doing things that I know are not good or productive. I don't want to be doing them, but I do them anyway. Either that, or I end up doing nothing at all. There is a part of me which remembers how I am when I am feeling well, and is desperately trying to get back to that version of me, but it does not succeed; I'll be coming back to that idea later in this book. For now, I want to concentrate on the larger picture. People might see some of the outward effects. A few might even start to put the pieces together, and recognize them as a pattern which suggested some kind of mental illness. My overall inner experience, however, is the feeling that my own mind is betraying me.

The disciples in the upper room are shocked at the very idea that one of them will betray Jesus. After all, they were his trusted inner circle. He had called them all to follow him, and they had done so, leaving their lives behind. Jesus had taught them. They had seen him do marvelous, incredible things. They had come to believe that he was the Messiah, the Christ, God's chosen savior of his people. They knew also that he was seen as trouble, especially by some of the religious authorities. They must have known that he was at risk, and therefore so were they. But the idea that one of them would betray him? It was almost beyond belief—though as Jesus and Judas both knew, it was already coming true even as he spoke.

My mind betrays me. It lets me down. It turns me over to dark, dangerous forces which I would rather not face. By the time I recognize it, it is already happening. To begin with, my experience was not that of Jesus, who is actively choosing not to stop the betrayal because he is embracing the fate which awaits him as the climax of his mission. Nor was it that of Judas, the proactive agent of the betrayal. It was more akin to the experience of the rest of the disciples; shock, confusion, and fear at something which is beyond their control, something which is already taking place even as it is named.

As anyone unfortunate enough to experience it will know, it is a painful thing to be betrayed by somebody you trust. In fact, you can only be betrayed by somebody you trust. If you didn't trust them already, then it isn't really a betrayal—so every betrayal comes with pain. Even Jesus, as sure of his destiny as he was, must have felt that pain. He was human, after all. Some of those who commit betrayals at least do so for an obvious gain; Judas did get his thirty pieces of silver. When my mind betrays me, it is for no gain at all. Quite the opposite, in fact; there is only loss. And it is painful. Just as with betrayal by another person, trust is broken. Except now it was my own mind which I no longer trust. At a quite fundamental level, mental illness has caused me to lose trust in myself.

Following my diagnosis, I slowly became more familiar with what was happening to me. Eventually, I suppose I became a little more like Jesus in this vignette, inasmuch as I became more alert to the reality of what was happening, rather than being taken by surprise. Not only did I become more aware of how and when mental illness was affecting me detrimentally, but I became more adept at coping with it. It was not a question of stopping it, for nothing could stop it; but I could minimize the worst of its effects, and discipline myself to continue functioning relatively well during all but the darkest times of the shadow. For me, that meant managing my workload sensibly to allow time for rest and recovery, cutting down on some social interaction, and taking more time to do things which I knew I enjoyed—crucially, even if I didn't actually feel any sense of enjoyment at that moment. It included a lot of walking. Being outside in the fresh air is a tried and trusted weapon against depression for good reason; it often works. Not infallibly, and not alone, but it does work.

I suppose I also became accustomed to the sense of betrayal. The feelings of shock and pain became dulled with horrible familiarity, though they were never absent. That continuous presence in itself became another shadow. I lived with the reality that my mind could let me down again at any moment, and I found that this began to cast its shadow over everything, even when I wouldn't say that I was feeling ill. When you have been betrayed by another person, you are naturally more guarded around them. You might not share confidences with them. You might not give them weighty responsibilities like you did. One way or another, the natural reaction is to limit the amount of trust you place in that person, for fear that they will betray that trust again.

Now imagine what that is like with your own mind. Or perhaps you don't need to imagine it, because you have been there just as I have. The difference is that you have no choice except to trust your own mind, even though you don't want to. So you end up always fearing betrayal, even when betrayal is not actually happening. That is a big burden to live with; indeed, the fear of mental illness is sometimes as much of a struggle and burden as the mental illness itself. Once the trust you have with your own mind is broken, as mine is, it takes a very long time to rebuild. It might not even be possible to rebuild it at all.

For some people, that burdensome lack of trust becomes overwhelming, and leads to suicide as a way to end a seemingly intolerable situation. Every suicide is a tragedy, and it is surely incumbent on us as societies to explore our means of support so that fewer people die this way, even if we are unlikely to manage to reduce that number to zero. However, though much too common, suicide is rare. Most people who experience this betrayal of the mind, like me, find ways to learn to live with it. We develop coping mechanisms, we become more adept at recognizing our limitations, more alert to the need for self-care. In short, we get used to being betrayed. You end up building in the possibility of betrayal to your planning. That approach certainly worked for me, more or less. Mental illness just became a part of who I was—a sometimes tiresome and annoying part, but something that was just there. The vicissitudes of my mental health didn't really stop me any more, even if they might occasionally slow me down a little; until the moment when I was, suddenly and forcefully, stopped in my tracks.

Sudden strike

Suddenly, one of those with Jesus put his hand on his
sword, drew it, and struck the slave of the high priest,
cutting off his ear.—Matt 26:51

O NE SUMMER'S DAY, I went from the vicarage to our small parish office space in the next village, about three miles away.
There was a recalcitrant photocopier which needed some attention.
I was scheduled to take a call from the engineer which would hopefully help. As far as I know, that call never made it to me.

I say as far as I know, because arriving in the office is the last
thing I properly remember. Following that, I have some patchy
memories. I remember being in the emergency department of
the local hospital. I remember that I had frequent visits at home
from mental health professionals (though I can't tell you precisely
who, or why), and that the Bishop, the Archdeacon, and the Area
Dean also all visited, but I can't put those things in any kind of
order. My next properly placed memory is about a month later,
when we went as a family on a combined holiday and retreat to
the Society of Mary and Martha at Sheldon in Devon. Even after
that things are still somewhat hazy for another few weeks. What
I know of that time is in part because other people—my wife,
mainly—have told me about them, or by a process of deduction,
or a combination of both. I don't think the call from the photocopier engineer made it to me because I have found out since that
other people spoke to the company in order to solve the problem,
and nobody has hinted that the original call got through.

I know now that I drove home from the office, though I don't remember doing so. I broke down in tears in my wife's study, telling her over and over "I can't do this". I know now that the visit to the emergency department happened about thirty-six hours after I arrived back home, following several telephone calls between my wife and various departments of the National Health Service, and that the reason was to rule out any physical problems. I know now that I became very upset and angry when it was suggested that I needed to go into the department alone, because of the protocols in place due to the Covid-19 pandemic (in the end, they allowed my wife to accompany me throughout). I know now that I spent most of the next few weeks constantly asking my wife, "What should I be doing?"

The truly scary thing is that I know all of that now, but I only know it because I have been told. I remember none of it.

Perhaps the only thing which I do remember from that time is the feeling which was prompting me to ask constantly about what I should be doing. I was experiencing an overwhelming urgency that there were jobs to do, tasks to accomplish, but I simply could not access what they might be. As a parish priest, the list of things to do is basically never ending. However much you do—and at that time I frequently "worked" seventy hours or more a week—there is always something else that you could do, perhaps even should do. You need to set your own limits in an otherwise unlimited job, something at which I was not always very good. So there would certainly have been plenty of things which, had I been well, I would and should have been doing. I guess that my mind simply shut them all away from me, leaving me with the sense that I should be doing something and no idea what that something was.

Given that I was simultaneously terrified of the telephone ringing or the door knocking, that I was desperate to avoid people, and unable to concentrate or focus on anything, I have no idea how or why I thought I could actually do any of those mystery things. But in those first few weeks, I was possessed by a feeling of needing to be busy, though with no connection to any actual task, and no ability to perform those tasks even if

somebody had told me what they were. It was a little like press-
ing the accelerator to the floor in a car which is running but in
neutral; there is a lot of noise and the engine spins very fast, but
unless you engage a gear it will never go anywhere. My mind was
spinning, noisily and frantically; but it wasn't engaged, couldn't
find anything to engage, so it wasn't going anywhere at all. In
the meantime, what I needed was constant reassurance that there
wasn't actually anything I should be doing.

It took about a month for my mind to calm down enough so
that I started to change. I realized how ill I was, and therefore how
very ill I must have been. With that realization came increasing ac-
ceptance that there was nothing I should be doing, indeed there was
very little which I could do. I still feared the possibility of having
to interact with people outside of my immediate household. I had
very limited powers of concentration. Rest and quiet, along with the
prescribed medication, were the order of the day.

With that slowly increasing self-knowledge, however, came
increased fear. This had been an unpredicted, catastrophic betrayal
by my mind. I had completely shut myself down, and I could not
find a reason why. That was very scary. What if it happened again?
Would I ever be able to return to work, and what would happen
to my family if I couldn't? Would I ever actually get better, or was
something inside me now broken beyond repair?

The blow which cuts off the ear of the servant of the high
priest is sudden, and unexpected. It is the suddenness, as much
as the violence itself, which makes it such a shocking moment in
the story, albeit one which is often left unremarked as we (understandably) focus rather more on the violence which is to come in
the crucifixion, but it is worth taking a moment to think about
what happens here. I don't think there is any equivalent or parallel
act of physical violence anywhere else in the gospels. Lashing out
in this way seems to be entirely out of character for any of the
disciples. It seems to be the desperate act of someone who is convinced that they need to do something, but has no idea what to do

for the best. There is actually little chance it could have changed things; one may imagine that the servant of the high priest was not exactly the lynchpin of the plan to arrest Jesus. It certainly goes against not only the Lord's teaching, but also his plan for how things are going to unfold, indeed for how they must unfold for God's loving purposes to be revealed.

In a similar way, while it would be easy for me to focus only on the profound illness which lasted for months, I cannot escape the fact that the suddenness of the onset has itself left an indelible mark on me. I had become accustomed to recognizing the moments of slow betrayal early, and dealing with them. Here, by contrast, I don't feel that I had a clue what was going to happen before it did. I was, as far as I could tell, absolutely fine—a little stressed, perhaps, but not to an unusual or extreme degree—right up until the moment where I was suddenly became very unwell. It was unexpected by me and by everyone else, and violently sudden. I couldn't deal with it.

As I began to recover, the idea that I might no longer be able to manage my own mental health became a real worry. If something this sudden had happened once, then surely it could happen again. This new, sudden type of betrayal would be more than I could handle if it turned out to be more than a one-off event. I had learned to live with recognizing the signs and managing them; but if there were no longer going to be signs to recognize, and if the results were going to be this catastrophic, it was difficult to see how I could go on in any meaningful way.

That feeling is where my story and this brief violent vignette from the gospels diverge. The attack by the disciple on the slave of the high priest makes no actual difference to the outcome of events, inasmuch as it does not prevent Jesus' arrest—and in Luke's narrative, Jesus heals the slave, so in the end it doesn't make a lasting physical difference to him either. It is a shocking moment, yes, but it is over as soon as it has begun, and of no real consequence to what follows. For me, by contrast, the shock of this sudden strike of significant mental illness took on a life of its own within the illness, especially as I began to recover. One cannot help but wonder how the high priest's slave felt about people with swords afterwards.

It was only with the benefit of hindsight, and the help of a wise and lovely counsellor, that I began to make sense of what had happened. I had been living and ministering through a very stressful time, as we all coped with the opening months of the Covid-19 pandemic. The rules imposed by the UK government and the Church of England authorities alike were restrictive, complex, rapidly changing, and often without any discernible reason or logic. It had involved a complete re-invention of how to be a parish priest, and the rapid acquisition of a whole new digital skill set. Then, in the final weeks before the sudden onset of my illness, there had been the news that we would be able to return (albeit in a limited way) to worshipping in person in church buildings— news which brought with it another complex and rapidly changing set of rules and guidelines, and a new level of both expectation and worry from many parishioners, in both cases sometimes completely out-of-touch with reality.

I saw it as my role to attempt to hold all of this together. In many ways I felt that I had no choice but to accept that role. Some of the legislation and guidance was issued so late to deadlines that I often felt that I had to take some quite big decisions alone and accept the consequences afterwards, because there was simply no time to consult if we were to comply with them. I must be calm, I was thinking. I must not show that I am ruffled, or stressed. I must show spiritual and social leadership, even though I am prevented from all my usual ways of doing so.

Of course, the truth is that I, like so many others, was completely out of my depth, with no real idea what to do, just making it up as I went along and hoping for the best. I was not calm, and I was stressed—but unlike other times, when I had learned to be attuned to those feelings and take care of them and myself, I was blocking it all out. This was partly a conscious decision, but also partly subconscious. When public worship re-started, the ever-changing guidance for how it should be conducted, coupled with some less-than-charitable behavior on the part of a few parishioners, proved to be too much. The insignificant problem with the photocopier was simply the final straw.

The sudden strike I encountered was not, in fact, completely out of the blue as I had first thought. Rather, it was the breaking of a dam which had been holding back months of ignored and repressed stress. Unable to cope with being ignored any longer, the part of my mind which tended to betray me had given up hinting at me, and had forcefully shut me down.

Perhaps the experience of the disciple was similar. Particularly in the last days leading up to his crucifixion, we might fairly imagine that life with Jesus was far from dull. The disciples had come to trust and respect him as their Lord and Teacher, to see in him the Messiah, God's anointed who would save their people. The heightened emotions of the entry into Jerusalem only a few days previously had been ramped up even further as Jesus cleansed the Temple, radically subverted the Passover meal with the declaration that the bread and wine were his own body and blood, and announced his own betrayal. It is worth remembering too that it was now late at night—so late that the disciples were struggling to stay awake. A mob arrives, led by somebody whom the disciples would have considered one of their own. It is easy to see that this has turned into a highly stressful situation, and easy to imagine the disciple losing control of his emotions and actions for a moment. Having tried so hard to hold things together for so long, he quite literally lashes out, apparently without thought for the damage or the consequences. Similarly, my mind had little concern for the damage which might be caused to me or to those around me, or for the consequences of what was happening. Just as for the disciple in the Garden of Gethsemane, it was all too much. Something had to be done. Things needed to be stopped. I needed to be stopped.

What is truth?

Jesus answered, "For this I was born, and for this I came
into the world, to testify to the truth. Everyone who be-
longs to the truth listens to my voice." Pilate asked him,
"What is truth?"—John 18:37b–38a

T RUTH IS, I THINK, quite a slippery thing. The same event
might produce quite different versions of the "truth" depending on the perspective of the narrator. Indeed, I am told that
the police, for instance, consider it suspicious if the various accounts of eyewitnesses to an incident correspond too precisely.
One imagines that historians in Germany, the UK, and the USA,
all tell the story of the Second World War slightly differently,
though equally truthfully. The Gospels themselves are evidence of
this—four accounts of the ministry of Jesus which, while clearly
telling the same overall story of the same person, differ from each
other. The four Evangelists each have different priorities they
want to communicate, different themes of Jesus' ministry which
they want to draw out. No lies, but four different versions of the
truth, and we are richer for having all of them.

Things can also be "true" in non-literal ways. I believe that
the beginning of Genesis tells us real and important truths about
the network of relationship between God, humanity, and the
whole created order. I don't believe that the universe went from
nothing to everything in 144 hours (and neither do the vast ma-
jority of other Christians). Genesis 1 is not literally 'true' in the
sense of communicating scientific facts, but it does tell us other

theological and sociological things that are true. Creative arts such as poetry often function in a similar way; in some circumstances it really is the case that "beauty is truth, truth beauty". If it were not, Keats would surely not have composed a whole poem about a vase in order to make that point.

So Pilate was not just being facetious when asking "What is truth?" It is an honest question, especially when Jesus is being particularly enigmatic in a situation where one imagines that most people would be desperately trying to demonstrate their innocence. Jesus wasn't about to lead the armed rebellion against Rome which some wanted him to and others feared he would, but that didn't mean that he wasn't (and isn't) "King of the Jews" in other ways. As Pilate himself puts it of that title later in the story, "What I have written, I have written". There is a recognition that therein lies truth, even if it is not the whole truth.

The fact that multiple perspectives yield multiple versions of the truth, and that things can be true on different levels, doesn't mean that truth is entirely relative—at least, I don't think so. I am instinctively wary of the modern trend towards privileging "my truth". Just because I might say or think something doesn't automatically make it true. Some things are not true, and don't become true just because I say or wish they are. Lies are real, and they are false. That's really important, because mental illness tells you some horrible lies about yourself.

Perhaps it might be more accurate to describe my experience as a loss of confidence in my ability to distinguish truth and lies about myself. As I write this, I know which of what follows is truth and which is lies, but sometimes in the grip of illness I begin to believe that the lies are actually the truth. When I am well, for example, I know that even when difficult times come, I will get better. Sometimes I can hold on to that when things are difficult. Sometimes, however, I can't, and I begin to believe the lie my mind is telling me that I will be stuck in the doldrums for ever. I might begin to believe a more pernicious lie, that I don't deserve to recover. Occasionally (and for me this has been thankfully rare, though I know full well that for others it is a horribly common occurrence) I have ended up believing that it would be better if I simply ended it all; better for me, and better for those close to me. That lie is very dangerous when you begin to believe it as truth. And because you have begun to believe it as truth, you begin to think that people who are telling you the actual truth—that you are loved, that you matter, that you can be helped to get better—are lying to you.

There are other distortions of the truth as well, not just that massive existential one. Sometimes I will feel that I can, and should, be carrying on as normal even when I am feeling unwell, or conversely that I am capable of doing nothing at all. It is almost always the case that neither of those things is true. For me, completely stopping is rarely the best option, as it tends to leave me wallowing in my own misery, thereby making things worse rather than better. Nevertheless, carrying on as normal involves ignoring warning signs and putting myself at risk of more serious illness—and as I have already tried to explain, I discovered that the hard way. If when you are ill you believe the lie that you are not, and that you simply need to knuckle down and get through it, that can end up being quite dangerous in its own way, and certainly counterproductive. If you need to slow down, then do it early and in a controlled way, because sooner or later your mind and body will force it upon you.

The smaller lies include the lies of comparison, the thoughts which tell you that you are a failure because other people are coping fine when you are not, or that there are lots of people worse off than you so you have no right to be suffering. These are, of course, mingled with a grain of truth. There almost certainly are people who are in worse situations than you are. But that's not how mental illness works, any more than it is how physical illness works. You can try and avoid being in situations or doing things which might make you ill, you can take actions you know will keep you healthy, but there are no guarantees. Non-smokers get lung cancer. Athletes die of unexplained heart failure. It may well be true that you are not in the worst possible situation in the world, but it is a lie that you should therefore not be suffering from mental illness. I'll be reflecting a little more on the challenges of comparison later on.

That was certainly the case for me. In many ways I was very comfortable, far more so than a lot of people during the Covid pandemic. I had a good job and good job security, a consistent, predictable and comfortable income, and (thanks to the nature of most Church of England vicarages, which come with the job) a better house than I could ever dream of affording if I had to buy it myself. None of my family were ill or in particular need. Yes, the pandemic had made my job more difficult and more stressful, but I was hardly alone in that experience. None of that made any difference. Other people coped, other clergy coped. I did not.

And so the next lie is that you are a failure, that your mental illness is a sign of weakness or some other deficiency, a signal that you are not good enough at your job, that you have let down your family and those close to you. In the first few weeks of my shutdown that was not an issue for me, because (as I've said) I simply couldn't access thoughts about what I should or should not be doing. As I began to slowly recover, however, I felt enormous amounts of guilt. I felt like I had failed my family and my parishioners. I felt like I had failed God. Those feelings were only exacerbated when I eventually found it necessary to leave that post, even though my experience of mental illness was not the prime reason for leaving. I knew intellectually that mental illness was not the same as weakness, that it was not failure, but that knowledge makes no difference in the crucible of actually experiencing illness. Even writing this now, quite some time after the event, I can feel that sense of failure returning. Of all the lies your mind tells you, I have found that one the hardest to shake off. I am not sure I entirely have done so. Perhaps I never quite will. That's the problem with the lies of mental illness—they can become the truth in their own way. Pilate's question always remains a relevant and apt one.

Ecce homo

> When Pilate heard these words, he brought Jesus out-
> side and sat on the judge's bench at a place called The
> Stone Pavement, or in Hebrew Gabbatha. Now it was
> the day of Preparation for the Passover; and it was
> about noon. He said to the Jews, "Here is your King!"
> —John 19:13–14

"HERE IS YOUR KING!" In much older translations of the
Bible, Pilate's display of Jesus was accompanied by the
words "Behold the man!"—in the Latin of the Vulgate, *Ecce homo*.
I've never found it quite clear what Pilate's motive was for bringing Jesus in front of the crowds in this way. Was it to humiliate
Jesus? Or was it to show the crowds that he was just an ordinary
man, not a revolutionary and therefore no threat to Rome? Pilate
always seems to me to be desperately (but unsuccessfully) trying
to find a way of not executing Jesus. Is this public moment an
invitation to a lynching, or a last roll of the dice to try and get
Jesus off? Either way, and whatever words Pilate did or didn't
actually say, there is no doubt that Jesus is on very public display.
Whether he goes to his death or walks free, the crowd will be
talking about only one person today. Pilate must have known
that. Jesus must have known that.

Mental illness is apparently still seen by many as something
of a taboo subject. It is something we apparently just don't talk
about. I don't think that is true. In fact, I don't think it has ever
been true; if my experience is anything to go by, I think that mental

illness and the people who suffer with it have always been talked about, albeit usually in hushed and ignorant tones.

At one point in my recovery—sufficiently far into my recovery that I was back to at least some ministerial duties—I ended up at the Maundy Thursday Chrism Mass at the cathedral. Covid-19 meant that there could only be a small congregation there in person, so the relative anonymity often afforded by cathedral worship (especially on occasions such as this when it would normally be full) wasn't an option. It was easy for everyone present to see who else was there.

I spent the whole service becoming increasingly convinced that everyone had seen me, that they all knew I had been ill for a long time, and that they were all talking about me. Of those three aspects, the first was inevitable with such a small congregation. The second might have had some grain of truth to it—I was in a small diocese, and word does get around. The third, the idea that everyone was talking about me, was the damaging one; it's also the one which almost certainly wasn't true.

I didn't think that nobody was talking about mental illness. It would have been much better for me if I did think that. On the contrary, I was convinced that everyone was talking about me, and my illness. In my mind, that wasn't a positive thing. I found the experience of that service very unpleasant, and not at all worshipful. Surely, I thought, the talk would just be negative and critical. "There's David", I imagined my colleagues and friends saying. "He just can't cope". "I don't know why he is still here". And remember, this was my state of mind quite some time (eight months or so) after I had been my most ill. This was how I was thinking when I was sufficiently recovered as to be back working and in public view.

Conversely, it was probably about eight weeks after I had first become ill that I decided to say something to the congregations in my care about the fact that I was suffering with mental illness. Up until that point they had simply been told that I was unwell, and that it was uncertain when I would be returning to duties. With the Covid-19 pandemic raging, I felt that I had to make some kind of statement about the nature of my illness in order to quash any speculation there might have been that I was Covid-stricken—in particular to allay any suspicion that I might have been interacting with parishioners while contagious. Rightly or wrongly, I felt that I owed people at least the outlines of an explanation of my ill health.

I don't remember the possibility that it would get people talking about me crossing my mind. To me, it was all about shutting down the idea that everyone was talking about me. I don't know if it was something which I needed to do or not, because I had no actual information about whether or not people were talking about me. I also don't know whether it stopped them talking about me. I never shook the idea that they might be. I suppose that is part of being a public figure like a vicar—whether you like it or not, your life seems to become public property. Most of the time that is fine, if occasionally a little annoying, though it can be harder on the family than it is on you. But when there is a real problem, such as being ill, it can become a bit of a nightmare, particularly if (as in my case) your illness leaves you feeling particularly vulnerable and exposed. For good or ill, I felt obliged to say something publicly. At the time, I just accepted it as a reality. Looking back, I don't think it is a very healthy or helpful situation in which to find yourself.

The lasting impact of the anxiety element of my illness, which remained long after the initial state of helplessness, was a fear of encountering other people. I hated the sound of the telephone ringing or the door knocking. It was about a month before I was able to leave the house at all, and even then I needed to have somebody with me. It was much longer before I felt able to walk into the village (again, only with somebody with me) where I was highly likely to encounter somebody I knew. In the first few weeks I was visited only by mental health professionals. After that there was a careful branching out to a few key church people—the bishop, the archdeacon, a trusted churchwarden—but I always needed my wife there, and I found such visits highly stressful and very tiring.

This high state of anxiety remained even as the depressive aspects began to lift. It was anxiety, rather than depression, which set back my recovery on several occasions. It is still hanging around inside my mind; there are still times when I have to steel myself to answer the door, or when I feel the need to allow a call to go to the answerphone even though I am sat at my desk. All clergy get their fair share of grumpy or difficult emails, but I now find that they hit harder and that it takes a lot more time and thought to muster a suitable reply. I take medication which helps to alleviate the worst effects, and I am very grateful for that, but I am coming to the conclusion that I will never quite shake these last vestiges. When I have bad days, it is now as likely to be my anxiety as my depression which is troubling me. Over the years, I have become used to the specter of depression. Now I have another aspect of mental illness with which I need to learn to live.

I think that the nature of the role of clergy, and in particular clergy in parish ministry, leaves you feeling that you are 'on show' more than perhaps you actually are. Most of the time, you live in your parish (indeed, in the Church of England at least, you need the express permission of your bishop not to). That has a dual impact. Firstly, lots of people know where you live. Secondly, every time you step out of the front door you are, in a sense, "at work"—which is why Church of England clergy aren't paid a wage, we are paid a stipend, which is actually money not to work so that we can be free for the "work" of ministry. That's just the physical element. Your telephone number and your email address, at least your "work" ones, are also public property. Sometimes, the world feels like it is divided into two kinds of people: those who think you only work on Sundays, and those who can't conceive that you have days off and holidays. Sometimes it feels like both kinds of people expect immediate responses at all times.

If any of that sounds like a complaint, it isn't meant to. Anybody who is even considering ordination should know that this is what being a parish priest is like. You have to love people; which doesn't mean that you need to be an extrovert, life-and-soul-of-the-party type, but you do need to care deeply about them. You have to be able to cope with the unplanned, and with sudden "changes of gear" as you go from happy events to sad ones to tediously necessary ones and back again. You have to accept that, if you are inhabiting your role even vaguely properly, you will become a lightning rod for all sorts of complaints and troubles as well as good news. To borrow Kipling's phrase, you will meet with triumph and disaster, and in some ways you will need to treat them just the same. That's the nature of being a parish priest. And I loved it—but you can probably work out by now why it is that it hits especially hard when you are suffering with anxiety and depression as I did. Being a public figure, knowing that people know (or at least think they know) who you are and what you do and even where you live, knowing that opening the front door or answering the phone opens you up to the potential of who knows what, is really not compatible with anxiety-inducing mental illness. I am convinced that if I had been in a "normal" job, the kind where you go to an office or factory or shop or wherever, do your work, and then come home again, I would not have been as ill and I would have recovered more quickly, at least to a state of being functional. Instead, I ended up feeling like I was "on show" in the vulnerability of my illness. For quite a long time, I felt like I was always being seen even though I was desperate to hide. To be honest, I still have days like that. It was, and is, extremely unpleasant and uncomfortable. Behold the man at his most vulnerable, at his lowest and most difficult ebb, when his life is totally out of his own control.

Living waters

After this, when Jesus knew that all was now finished,
he said (in order to fulfil the scripture), "I am thirsty." A
jar full of sour wine was standing there. So they put a
sponge full of the wine on a branch of hyssop and held
it to his mouth.—John 19:28–29

I DON'T REALLY REMEMBER THE very early stages of my illness,
but I don't think I really knew that I was ill. Rather, I was just
coping, surviving moment to moment as best I could. The level of
self-knowledge required to know that I was unwell didn't really
materialize until a few weeks in.

At that point, I found myself vacillating between two
thoughts. One was that I was never going to recover, that this was
how I now was. I remember saying to one of the consultants I saw
when I was still very ill, "If this is as much as I recover, I think
I can live with it". Had that proved to be the case, it would have
been a shadow of my former life. I would have been more or less
trapped in the house, unless accompanied by my wife into other
non-threatening situations. My active ministry would certainly
have been over. But there were times when I genuinely thought
that was how things would turn out.

The other thought, the one I had more often, was the feeling of a desperate desire to go back to how things were before I
was ill. I didn't, however, have any idea of how I could do that; in
fact, I only had a dim impression of what life was like—what I was
like—before I became unwell. I can reflect now that it was a good
thing this was the dominant thought, because it meant that I was

at least motivated to recover, even if I couldn't work out how I was going to. It could have been very easy to allow the first thought, the resignation that I was never going to recover, to swallow me up. Had it done so, it would surely have become a self-fulfilling prophecy. It was a good thing that I wanted to be well again, even if I felt powerless to make it happen.

Powerlessness has its own power. Not over other people or situations, but over you. I think that is particularly the case when, like I experienced at that stage of my illness, you don't really know what it is that you want the power to accomplish. In any case, powerlessness leaves you particularly vulnerable. There is still power in that situation, but you don't hold any of it, and that leaves you open to risk and dependent upon others. Perhaps paradoxically, that reality itself exercises a power over you. It pins you in place, unable to help yourself. Being powerless has the power to keep you powerless.

Jesus' need on the cross was one of the most basic human needs. He was thirsty—he needed something to drink. But he was utterly powerless to quench that thirst, and was therefore utterly dependent upon what others might choose to do for him. Was the offer of sour wine a kindness, or a further taunt? Perhaps it was all that was available, and the bystanders judged it to be better than nothing; or perhaps it was a kind of joke to give criminals in that desperate situation something which would not slake their thirst but rather worsen it. In either case, Jesus' powerlessness to meet his own basic needs is compounded by his powerlessness to choose what help is (or is not) given to him.

What is truly remarkable, of course, is that Jesus is actively choosing this situation. To describe God the Son incarnate as "powerless" is at one level fundamentally wrong. Jesus healed the sick and raised the dead; he fed the multitudes and commanded even the wind and waves. His infinite power is limited only by his choosing to limit it. Here at the cross is revealed the great extent of the limits he is at every moment choosing for himself. In John 5, Jesus speaks with the Samaritan woman at the well of his gift of "living water", the water that those who drink of it will never be thirsty—yet here, he thirsts. Just as at the beginning of his ministry he is not tempted to turn stones into bread to feed his hunger, at this moment he will not quench his own thirst. For us, powerlessness has its own power over us. For Jesus, powerlessness is perhaps the supreme exercise of his own power, for he has at all times the absolute and complete power to choose.

I think, in fact, that the desire to be well again was the first inkling that I was not, in fact, powerless. I wanted to be well, even though I felt like I had no idea what 'well' was. Jesus knew that he was thirsty, even though he (through his own choice) did not have the power to do anything to remedy that need. After several weeks, I had come to the self-knowledge that I was unwell and needed to recover, even though I felt that I had no idea how to do so. My true powerlessness had in fact lain in those first days and weeks, when I did not know what was happening and was utterly dependent on others. I was not thirsty for recovery at that time; I had no concept that recovery was even necessary, much less an idea of what it was. The thirst for recovery only came with the realization that I was ill.

To encounter Christ and to receive the gift of living water, one first needs to realize that one is thirsty and in need of that water. The Samaritan woman in John 5 had come to draw water from the well. She knew her need of it. And when Jesus speaks of living water, she asks for that as well. She knows her needs. She knows that she needs this living water, even if (as we discover as the conversation continues) she is not entirely sure what it is or what it entails to begin with. Only later do the people of her city recognize Jesus as "the Savior of the world". Just as I did not realize that I needed recovery because I lacked the self-awareness to know I was ill, so too will we not seek the living water if we lack the self-awareness to know that there is something missing in our lives, something for which we thirst.

Unlike most physical illnesses, it is one of the scourges of mental illness that it is possible to be so ill that you do not even realize you are ill. Although I had lived with mental illness for my entire adult life, this was the first time I had found myself in that position. My greatest need for healing was at the point in which I had no idea that healing was even necessary, much less what it might look like. I look back on it now with genuine fear, praying that I will never experience it again. Once I knew that I was ill, I was able to take the important first step of wanting to get back to my dimly-remembered old life, even if I had no idea about how to get there. I had become thirsty for something.

The same can be true of any of us in a spiritual sense. It may well be that the living waters are lacking in our lives; but if we do not know that we are thirsty, or if we will not admit it to ourselves, we can hardly expect that thirst to be quenched. It will not be done to us without our wanting it. God offers and persuades, but does not compel. If we look in the wrong places we might find sour wine rather than pure water—but that is at least a start, because we know that we are looking for something. Arriving at the point of the awareness that I needed and wanted to recover was actually a significant turning point in my recovery phase, though I did not realize it at the time. Whether our needs be physical, mental, emotional, or spiritual, the first step to meeting them is to cry out from our positions of vulnerability, helplessness, and dependence; to know and to cry that we are thirsty.

Into your hands

Then Jesus, crying with a loud voice, said, "Father, into your hands I commend my spirit." Having said this, he breathed his last.—Luke 23:46

S O MANY KINDS OF illness, mental illness included, have the effect of dramatically increasing your dependence on other people. In the early days of the acute crisis I have described, I would barely eat or drink unless it was put in front of me, though as long as I was well-supplied I hadn't really lost my appetite as such. As I have said previously, I also needed constant reassurance that there was nothing (and in particular nothing work-related) that I should be doing. Of course, I was initially so ill that I lacked the self-awareness to understand that this was the situation, but that did not last. In fact, perhaps one of the first things I realized was just how much I was depending on others, and in particular my wife.

That brought with it a whole new set of complicated emotions. I loved my wife for taking care of me, and I was also amazed that she—that anybody—would do it for me. But above all I felt guilty that I was seemingly unable to look after myself properly, guilty for the strain I knew it must be placing on her.

This was all very different to an earlier experience of being very dependent on other people. Some eight years previously, I spent about three weeks in hospital having suffered a collapsed lung. Again, I was therefore dependent on other people to do things like bringing me food, and even for a while on machines to help me breathe properly. It was certainly a very frustrating experience, and frankly at times a quite boring one. But I certainly didn't have that same guilty feeling. In part, I think, there was a bit of selfishness of being able to dismiss the help I needed as people "just doing their jobs", though I was still grateful that they were doing their jobs. But in part, I think it was also because I knew and understood what was happening to me at every point. At times it was painful, annoying, and even scary, but I never experienced that detachment from reality which I would later with mental illness.

Jesus has already conceded in the garden that the divine will of the way of the cross, rather than his understandably human wish to avoid the suffering to come, must prevail. Here, as he breathes his last, he commends himself to the Father.

Doctrinally speaking, this gets a little complex and more than a little cloudy. Christian orthodoxy is that Jesus in the incarnation was possessed of two wills—the one divine will of the Trinity, and also a human will, the latter choosing always to be perfectly obedient to the former. Maximus the Confessor used the story of the agony in Gethsemane to argue and illustrate this very point. Since we believe that the crucifixion is divinely willed, and that Jesus is possessed of that divine will, it follows that Jesus goes to the cross willingly; but if he is sharing in one divine will, that makes some of the last words from the cross even more difficult to interpret. If Jesus and the Father are one (John 10:30), how can Jesus commend his spirit to the Father's keeping?

I don't know the answer to that question—and even if I did, this would not be the time or place to dive into what would undoubtedly be some complex and subtle theological treatise. Unlike my experience of mental illness, Jesus certainly knows what is happening to him. However, what I do recognize is that sense of being in a position of such extreme vulnerability and suffering that your only option is to hand your whole existence over to others, in the hope that they will keep it safe for you.

That placing of your life into someone else's hands, no matter how much you trust that person, is risky. It is risky for you, because you are giving up your independence and the power you have to make decisions for yourself. That may nevertheless be the least risky course of action, whether that be trusting an expert such as a stockbroker to make financial decisions on your behalf, trusting that the surgeon will act in your best interests while you are anaesthetized, or—as in my case and so many others of mental illness—simply losing the ability to make decisions for yourself. But it is still risky. It is also potentially risky for the person who assumes that responsibility. This is especially the case when it is caused by sudden illness, because that person has had no chance to prepare for the significant weight which is landing on their shoulders. At least the stockbroker and the surgeon both know what they will be doing when they head into work, and they both get to stop doing it when their shift is over. For my wife, and countless others like her, the burden is unexpected and inescapable.

I think that neither the church nor society generally is still very good when it comes to dealing with people who are suffering with mental illness. Campaigns to talk about it are all very well (though as I have already reflected, the idea that people were talking about me and my illness were unhelpful), but while I am sure that can be helpful to some people in some situations, it would not have made any difference to me or to many like me. What I think we are even less good at is dealing with the people who are left to pick up the pieces—the people into whose hands lives such as mine end up being placed. While support for me was patchy, it was at least attempted, certainly in the first weeks when I was at my most unwell. The support for my wife, who was bearing the brunt of my incapacity, was negligible. We simply must do better.

At least I was one of the lucky ones, in that my wife proved to have a very capable and strong pair of hands in this regard. I sometimes wonder what would have happened to me had I been single. I imagine that the damage to me and to whatever parishes I was serving would have been much more substantial. My ministry, not just in that place but generally, probably would not have survived; in all honesty, there is a chance that I would not have survived. That I am still here at all is thanks to a lot of people, including a whole variety of medical professionals, but is first and foremost down to my wife. Even though I was not consciously doing so, I commended my spirit into her hands.

I suppose I also commended my spirit into God's hands, though again I was not doing so consciously. I do know that other people were commending me to God in prayer as well. While I may have at times doubted my recovery, or my future ministry, one thing which may come as a surprise is that I never really questioned my faith. It's not that I have never questioned it under any circumstances, but I didn't do so in this particular circumstance. Perhaps it is in the nature of belief and trust in God that, although we may have doubts, those doubts don't surface at the most testing times, at the moments when faith and trust are all we have left. I wonder if that is what was behind this last word of the Lord from the cross. When nothing else is left, when all is finished, Jesus—more so than anyone else who has ever lived— knows that the Father's hands are strong and steady and waiting in love to receive him.

The walking dead

The tombs also were opened, and many bodies of the saints who had fallen asleep were raised.—Matt 27:52

I F I AM BEING honest, this is the one part of the crucifixion account I find very difficult to take literally. One imagines that dead people coming out of their tombs and walking around would provoke a lot of comment. It certainly wouldn't be forgotten. Personally, I would expect to find mention of it in Jewish and Roman accounts of the period. One surely cannot argue that it would be an unimportant event, unworthy of record and recall. There is also the unresolved question of what happened to the dead subsequently. Did they die again? Or was this the beginning of the general resurrection, in which case are they still living? Or were they assumed bodily into heaven (and if so, why isn't that recorded)?

I am not the kind of person who easily dismisses the gospel accounts as allegory or metaphor. I believe that the gospels record actual events and actual teaching surrounding an actual person, Jesus of Nazareth. I have no problem at all believing in his literal physical resurrection, nor in the miracle by which he brought Lazarus back to life. But the idea that multiple simultaneous resurrections in a busy city would pass without comment by contemporary historians of the period, nor indeed be mentioned in all the gospels, just seems a bit far-fetched to me; so I am sorry, but I am reluctantly going to chalk this one up to Matthew's theological imagination.

But let us suppose that it did happen. Just imagine being in Jerusalem that day! People to whom you thought you had said goodbye forever, suddenly re-appearing in your life. There would be reunions of family and friends, surely joyous events after the initial shock had passed. However, it does not take much thought to realize that not every re-acquaintance with the past would be a happy one. There would be enemies—or if not enemies, at least people you would prefer to avoid. There would be reminders of past hurt and trauma which you thought you had dealt with and quite literally buried, only to be shockingly confronted with them once more. Reunions with a corrupt business partner, a disgraced family member, or a jilted ex-lover would be unlikely to be joyous in any context, but certainly not in this incredible one where you might reasonably have thought you would never see them again. "The saints" in a New Testament context usually means something like "everybody who believes in God", but that does not automatically mean they were (or are) all wonderfully delightful people whom everyone is pleased to see. One does not have to spend very long in church circles to discover that there are some unpleasant people there, as there are everywhere. There are certainly people whom I would have to regard as "saints" by that biblical definition, but whom I would be quite glad not to encounter again. Perhaps that is a failing of mine, but I don't think I am alone in that. I readily acknowledge that there are almost certainly people out there who would say the same about me.

Part of my experience of the depressive aspects of my mental illness was the very vivid recollection, almost resurrection, of so many moments and feelings from my past. Sometimes, it was a reminder of mistakes I had made, times where I felt I had got things wrong, occasions on which I had made a bad decision. Professional misjudgments and failings. Relationships gone sour, or not pursued out of fear. Look at yourself, they seemed to say. Look at all the darkness in your life; look at the darkness you have created for yourself and others. You are a worthless wreck of a man. You don't deserve to be well, let alone happy or successful.

Other times, they were what one might call highlights. Times when I had felt especially loved or wanted, and memories of the people who loved and wanted me at those times. Moments of achievement, success, and satisfaction. These are the kinds of thoughts and memories which when all is fine make you smile, and spur you on. But in illness they too become taunts; this is who you used to be, but you aren't that person any more, and you never will be. For you, joy and pleasure are gone, never to return.

One of the traps I have found in mental illness is that the bodies of my past are raised and start walking around my present, sometimes to the point of controlling it. What is more, my experience of all of those memories, be they objectively "good" or "bad", is overwhelmingly negative. One ends up trapped in a never-ending negative cycle, vividly re-living all the negatives as inevitable while dismissing the positives as impossibilities, which thus feeds itself (and you) more and more negativity—which of course only makes it harder to fight the depression which is causing this unvirtuous circle in the first place. And because you are overwhelmed by this endless replaying of memories—by these dead bodies walking around everywhere—it becomes very difficult to imagine any kind of future, much less a bright and happy one.

It is worth noting, I think, the complicated role which anti-depressant medication can play in these circumstances. More than once in my life, I have been grateful to have it as a much-needed support; but my experience is that it tends to "flatten out" my emotions. This does have the effect of making the negative things seem less bad, so I think that medication does the most good when you are trapped in the spiral of negativity I have described. However, it does also make the positive things seem less good, less life-giving, and therefore has the unfortunate effect of making it more difficult to imagine a bright future. I know that I am not the only one to have felt like this. I guess that, like any medical intervention, anti-depressants have their useful place. What is more difficult is judging if there is a point at which the downsides begin to outweigh the benefits.

With all these bodies walking around, it can be difficult to work out what to do next. Sometimes, the best option is simply to wait for them all to go back to where they belong—because eventually they will. Eventually your memories will go back to being just that, memories of the past, rather than a present torment. But sometimes, that can take a very long time. And sometimes, particularly if you are very ill, time may not be a luxury which you feel you have.

If you can find the energy (both mentally and physically), there is the option of pushing past them into the space beyond. Seizing the present opportunity, particularly if it is something at which you are good and which you would normally enjoy, can help you to leave all those dead bodies behind. After that, denied of the opportunity to torment you, they tend to go quietly back to their proper places. However, it is important not to underestimate just what a monumental undertaking this is; and it is important that people around you don't underestimate it either. Pushing your way through those bodies is hard work. Mental illness is not something you can just "snap out of". Even if intellectually you know that the space beyond exists, it might not be in your power right now to get there. If that is the case, don't worry. You have not failed. There will be another opportunity to try again, and in the meantime there is always the chance that the bodies will simply go away of their own accord.

But sometimes, you can't wait and you can't push through. At this point, some people sadly just become overwhelmed and give up. The only other option is to fight where you stand, so that if things don't get better, at least they don't get worse. And if pushing past takes energy, then fighting is exhausting, all the more so because all of your memories are being presented in a negative light. What I personally have found, though, is that the act of fighting begins the act of healing. Slowly but surely, you begin to see the memories as they truly are, not as your illness is distorting them. Little by little, the fight gets easier. The bodies start going back to where they should be. (I wonder if that is part of the difference between mental illness as I have experienced it, and conditions like dementia. I find that the bodies of my memory gang up on me. My admittedly limited and non-expert observation of dementia patients is that, for the most part, the bodies are aimlessly wandering around, rather than specifically looking to cause trouble.)

All my memories, good and bad, are part of the tapestry of experience which makes me who I am. They are, if you like, the "saints" of my own interior life—all of them valuable, even if not all of them are particularly enjoyable. I need them all, because without them, I am not me. It's unfortunate that when there is an upheaval in my mental health that the bodies of these "saints" come out of their tombs and start walking around, and it's even more unfortunate that I experience all of this so negatively. But it is perhaps understandable that paradigm-shaking events tend to force things to be re-arranged. I'm still not sure that I believe Matthew about the Jerusalem tombs; but I wouldn't say it was impossible. If crucifying God is not paradigm-shifting enough to wake a few corpses, then I don't know what is.

Starting from emptiness

Early on the first day of the week, while it was still dark, Mary Magdalene came to the tomb and saw that the stone had been removed from the tomb. So she ran and went to Simon Peter and the other disciple, the one whom Jesus loved, and said to them, "They have taken the Lord out of the tomb, and we do not know where they have laid him."—John 20:1–2

O NE OF THE IMAGES my counsellor gave me to help understand what had happened to me was that of a filing cabinet. Imagine, she said, that your life is like a filing cabinet which is full of stuff. Some of it, perhaps even quite a lot of it, is neatly filed in the right place. Some of it has just been shoved in there. Some of it you go to and use quite regularly, while other parts of it are things you are keeping because you somehow feel they are important, but you don't use them any more. The effect of an acute mental illness such as I experienced is to empty the filing cabinet all over the floor. Nothing is any longer where it should be, or where you had put it. You have to start again, picking things up, examining them, and dealing with them bit by bit; mostly by putting them back in the filing cabinet, but sometimes by putting them in the bin and getting rid of them entirely.

Those who, like Mary Magdalene, had followed Jesus had pinned all their hopes on him. He was the one, they thought, the promised Messiah who would save God's people. With his death, those hopes seemed to have been quashed. Now, a few days later,

Mary is denied even her final acts of devotion to the Lord whom she loved, as she discovers that his body is no longer in the tomb. The emptiness of hope is compounded by the literal, physical emptiness of the tomb. Mary has no idea where the Lord is. All she knows in this moment is that she will need to somehow rebuild her life, and that she is starting from an empty nothing.

One of the most difficult bits of re-filling the filing cabinet is that it isn't always clear what should go back in where, or what needs to be discarded entirely. The resultant process of trial and error as you attempt to put your life back together means that sometimes things can go wrong again; but you have to start somewhere, and for me that somewhere was the ministerial context I was in at the time. I arranged everything else around that. As it turned out, that was a mistake.

It took several setbacks in my recovery to realize it was a mistake. The only solution, as it turned out, was to pretty much empty the filing cabinet again, except this time a little less violently. Such a drastic move took all the courage I could muster. I ended up resigning the living of my parishes without anywhere or anything lined up in replacement. It was a risky move, but in the end it was the only move I could make if I wanted to thrive. What it didn't provide was any clarity. If anything, doing this highlighted that the tomb was still very much empty.

That lack of clarity seems to be characteristic of the empty tomb. As broken as she presumably was by Jesus' death, Mary Magdalene still knew what to do. She knew that she could go to the tomb and perform those last sad duties of care for the man whom she had followed. Her life still had some order. The empty tomb, however, throws everything into confusion. All Mary knows is that she does not know what to do. She does not propose a course of action. She does not start a search for the body, or an enquiry of those around who may know something. All she can do is report desperately to the others that the tomb is empty, and that she does not know where Jesus is.

We know, of course, that the story does not end there. But confusion reigns for a while. Prompted by Mary's shocking news, Peter and the other disciple run to the tomb and also find it empty. They, likewise, are none the wiser about what is happening; in fact, scripture specifically tells us that "they did not understand" (John 20:9). The men leave, while Mary remains, weeping.

The realization of the empty chasm that mental illness, especially acute mental illness, has caused in the ordering of your life can rather sneak up on you—but when you do realize it, confusion reigns. As I discovered, you can't refill the filing cabinet exactly as it was, and nor can you do it quickly. As traumatic as all of the rest of the experiences of mental illness can be, I personally think that this experience of the mind's empty tomb is potentially the most challenging point of all. As I have already mentioned, there have been times when I have been so determined to restore order that I have tried to force things into spaces they will no longer fit, with the result that things needed taking out again. There have been other times when I have given up all hope of order, and have resigned myself to leaving my life strewn all over the floor, just as the men gave up and walked away in confusion. Neither approach is conducive to a good recovery.

Leaving everything strewn on the floor and giving up is not really a recovery at all, even if you can convince yourself that you are content with it. If you force things back into the filing cabinet in what are now the wrong places, you will only end up taking them out again—or worse, they will come bursting out again just as they did before, leaving you back where you started and frankly even more likely to just give up. What I find challenging is that both of those approaches give me what I often crave; quick answers. As my recovery began to gather pace, I was so desperate to move on and put the whole experience behind me that a quick answer was incredibly attractive. The main problem with those quick answers, it turns out, is that neither of them really work.

Most difficult, but in my view most effective, is to follow the example of Mary. We must wait at the mind's empty tomb, not to enjoy it or to accept it, but to see what happens next. The men left, and they did not see the Lord. Mary in her sorrow chose to remain, and she did. She was the first to glimpse how her life could be put back together in a new and exciting way. She was the first to discover that the empty tomb was good news, was the gateway to new life. What it was not was an easy answer.

Starting from emptiness takes courage and patience. I know, because for me it is still very much a work in progress. But I firmly believe that if any kind of true recovery from mental illness is going to be possible, that it has to start by embracing the mind's empty tomb—as confusing and upsetting as it may be—and seeing it not as an ending but as a new beginning. As Mary Magdalene found, that may take a while to become apparent, and it will not be a quick, easy or obvious process to accomplish. There is no point in going back to exactly how things were before, because my mind has made it forcefully clear to me that the old patterns simply do not work. Life starts again and anew here, even though figuring out what now goes where in the filing cabinet is a very difficult job indeed.

Noli me tangere

Jesus said to her, "Mary!" She turned and said to him in
Hebrew, "Rabbouni!" (which means Teacher). Jesus said
to her, "Do not hold on to me, because I have not yet
ascended to the Father."—John 20:16–17a

RECOGNIZING THAT YOU ARE re-filling the filing cabinet of your
life in a new way, starting from emptiness, involves accepting
that your old life is not coming back exactly how it was, however
much you might at times want it to. Indeed, to perform the re-
constructive task well involves accepting that some things which
used to take up a lot of space in the cabinet now only deserve a
little; it might well also involve discovering that things which were
formerly insignificant now become more important.

One example from my own experience is running. I was not a
great fan of physical education at school, and apart from occasionally kicking a football around at theological college I had moved
no faster than a brisk walk for about twenty years. But in the early
stages of my recovery from my acute mental health crisis, when I
was casting around for anything which might help, I decided to
have a go at running. I had heard lots of people say that it had
helped them, and I figured that I had nothing to lose. It really did
help me; and to my great surprise, I actually enjoyed it. And because I enjoyed it, I went more often and for longer. I am not fast
by running standards, and I never will be. But I now own a medal
for completing a 10km race, a possibility at which I would have
laughed for most of my life. What was a tiny and ignored thing

when it came out of the filing cabinet has now gone back in to a much more prominent and frequently used position.

That is quite a positive narrative, of something which is helpful and healthful taking on a new importance. The reverse is also true. In all honesty I still have quite significant bits of my life on the floor, because I know that some of them need to go back smaller than they were, and I am struggling to work out which ones or how small they might be. But what I have learned already through this experience, which has been painful at times, is that the one thing I cannot successfully do is to hold on to my previous ways of living. Thinking in the long term, I can see how that has the potential to be invigorating. I have the opportunity to re-build my life in a way which is better and more fulfilling than what has gone before, a way which hopefully will be closer to Christ's promise and desire of abundant life (John 10:10). In the short term, however, it is quite scary; as I have already reflected, such is the nature of starting from an empty and disorganized space. What is certain is that, whether I like it or not, things will not be how they were before.

I imagine that Mary, in her joy and relief at encountering the risen Jesus, also had a thought along the lines of "it's okay, things will be how they were before". If she did, Jesus puts her right immediately. Before, he could be held on to. People literally followed him around, clamoring for his touch. But whatever this new life is, it is not the old one. Obeying Christ's call to follow him is no longer going to be about a physical journey through the Palestinian wilderness. Jesus is not to be held on to. It cannot be as it was before, and the followers of Jesus must slowly but surely work out what that means. As the story of Thomas later in John 20 shows, that will not always be easy. But it is necessary—and in many ways, it is the task which the church still performs even to this day, as in their own way does each individual Christian. Following Jesus is not merely about keeping to a list of clearly-defined instructions (though there are some of those, and we would do well to keep to them). It is about the disposition of your whole life.

I think it is also a task which finds resonances in dealing with the aftermath of spells of mental illness. I am reluctant to call it recovery; in my experience, reconstruction is a far better word. Since things will not be how they were before, there is no point in trying to hold on to that version of yourself. If my experience is any guide, your own memory of previous versions of yourself is in any case unlikely to be accurate. It might be an idealized version, viewed through rose-tinted spectacles. It might be the opposite, a hideous caricature. In either case, there is little point in striving to return to those versions of you, since they never actually existed. It might seem hard or even counter-intuitive at the time, but it is surely better to grasp the new possibilities which the deconstructed life offers. Much like Mary with Jesus, holding on too tightly to what we had (or thought we had) in the past is not a solution.

Notice, however, that there is good reason why Jesus is not to be held on to. He is ascending to the Father. This is the promise that the future, although different in ways the disciples cannot yet imagine, will be better, and that in the end it will be infinitely better, because he is going to prepare a place for them and has promised that he will return for them (John 14). The road between where they are right now and where they will be with Christ will not be smooth, and the journey will not be without its wrong turns. It is a journey into the unknown, but it is a journey into the promise of something better.

The task of reconstruction in the aftermath of mental illness will surely be a more fulfilling process if we approach it in that same spirit—as a journey which, although it is into the unknown, is toward the promise of something better. You may wish that you weren't starting from this point, and I know that feeling. But as a wise clergy colleague said to me regarding the state of the church following the Covid pandemic, "we may wish we weren't starting from this position, but we are, and so this is where God will start with us". I think the same is true for us as individuals. However miserable our starting points may be, God will start with us in those very points. It will take time, and we won't always get it right on the first attempt, but we can believe—I think we need to believe—that our lowest and emptiest ebbs can be turned into the opportunity to journey into the promise of something better. But that cannot happen if we hold on too tightly to the past, be that real or imagined.

None of this is to say that wholesale changes of personality are needed. Each and every one of us is fearfully and wonderfully made by God, and that has always been true. It was true before and during our experiences of mental illness, just as much as afterwards. I am emphatically not suggesting that we entirely abandon our pasts. Jesus still is who Jesus was, Mary still is who Mary was, the disciples are all still who they were. Those things did not change for them, and they do not need to change for us. We are each who we are, and our whole lives are part of that rich tapestry. I am still the person I was before my mental health crisis, just as I am still the person I was before my first diagnosis many years previously; but I am also not that person, because none of us (whatever has or has not happened to us) are now who we were in the past. To live is to change. To live in Christ is certainly to change, not least because we are called constantly to repentance.

Reconstructing a life from emptiness may be difficult at times, but we are not exactly starting from nothing. All the bits of our lives are there, even if they are scattered haphazardly around. They may well be put back differently—they probably should be put back differently, or else we are surely setting ourselves up for more problems in the future—and there might be one or two things which are newly discovered and one or two others which need to be discarded entirely, but they are still for the most part the same pieces which were always there. What I learned that I could not do is to cling too tightly to what life had been like before. I tried a bit too hard to do that, and it didn't work.

Mary cannot now hold on to Jesus, because the resurrection has changed things and life needs rebuilding in a new and different way—but this Jesus who has found her in the garden is still the same Jesus she has been following until now. His promise of still greater glory to come, when he will take the faithful to be with himself in eternity, moves closer through the emptiness of the tomb, and the physical parting of the ascension which is soon to come. These better things are only possible by letting go of aspects of the life which they have shared until now. Perhaps there is a lesson there for all of us, even without the need for a dramatic intervention such as a mental health crisis; if we want the future to be better than the past, we cannot hold the past too tightly. Sometimes we need to be brave enough to let some things go.

Those dear tokens

He said to them, "Why are you frightened, and why do doubts arise in your hearts? Look at my hands and my feet; see that it is I myself."—Luke 24:38–39a

IN LINE WITH MOST of the Christian tradition, I firmly believe in an unchanging God. I think it is a necessity which is related to God's trustworthiness. A changeable God might decide that I am no longer loved. A changeable God might decide that I can no longer be forgiven. Only an unchangeable God gives me that certain hope. As Henry Vaughan wrote (and Hubert Parry memorably set to music), "none can thee secure but One who never changes". I also believe that God wants all people to be saved (1 Timothy 2:4), though I don't think that necessarily means that all people *will* be saved (or to put it another way: I think it is theoretically *possible* that Hell could be empty, but it is not *certain* that it is). I think those things in combination have particularly subtle theological implications surrounding the crucifixion.

The crucifixion of Jesus is an historical fact, and therefore an historical moment. One day, early in the First Century AD, Jesus was crucified. That is, if you like, the human element of the story. But the theological element is something altogether more complex—far more complex than we can fully understand. My own thoughts are something like this.

Since God wants all people to be saved, and humanity is saved through Christ's death and resurrection, it must be the case that the *effects* of the cross are not temporally confined. In other words, it

is not just people who lived in the time period following the crucifixion who may gain the benefits of God's grace poured out in that
event. The cross "operates" throughout all time. In a theological
sense, we might therefore say that Christ is always being crucified,
and that Christ always has been crucified.

That also makes sense of an unchanging God. It cannot be
the case that God only decided to save people who have lived since
the crucifixion. That's not what scripture teaches us. It would also
be entirely inconsistent with God's loving and merciful nature. It
is not in the nature of God to be arbitrary, and it is certainly not
in the nature of God to be confined by time. The atoning work of
Christ on the cross is the outworking and demonstration of God's
will for all humanity—and that always has been God's will, and
always will be God's will, since God does not change. Once again,
this suggests that the effects of the cross are universal throughout history. The crucifixion is not God's hurried attempt to fix an
unexpected problem. It is part of God's eternal plan for creation,
securing both our free will and our salvation. Humanity was, is,
and always will be, redeemed.

Since the theological effects of the cross are present to and
from eternity, surely it is possible that the physical effects are too?
Indeed, one might say that of the whole Incarnation. It is not that
over the course of three decades or so God learned how to be human (as I once unfortunately heard somebody preach), since God
does not change; it is that in the Incarnation humanity was united
with the Godhead to and from eternity. We may think in a similar
way about the crucifixion. The temporal, physical reality of the
death and resurrection of Jesus are the means by which the salvation of all is achieved, to and from eternity. Specifically, I want to
suggest, the wounds which Christ receives on the cross on that day
in time are part of his being as the eternal Son. God's unchanging
nature of forgiveness is bound up in God's own eternal knowledge
of what it is to be humanly wounded, and to humanly wound. It is
all part of the paradox of the Incarnation.

When Jesus shows the disciples the wounds in his hands and
his side, it is not just to offer a calling-card of recognition, a proof

that he is not an imposter or look-alike. In this new post-resurrection reality, where his appearances to the faithful confirm that he is no longer confined by human bounds of space and time, Jesus is revealing more of himself as he truly is—a true being which includes being wounded. In a human sense, his wounds were not there before the crucifixion, and then they were there. In a divine sense, Jesus has always had his wounds and will always have his wounds, since that intimate knowledge of woundedness is part of God's eternally unchanging nature. In the Incarnation, those wounds were hidden; but they were always there, because they always will be there.

The beauty of the reality that woundedness is part of the God-head is that it means our wounds are also taken up into God. No illness, injury, or suffering is beyond God's reach or God's heart. It also means that we are each known and loved as we are, rather than how we might wish to be. I find all of that to be a great comfort. When mental illness stops me loving myself, which it does quite often, God still loves me. On the thankfully much rarer occasions when it stops me even knowing myself properly, God still knows me. I am grateful that I have been able to hang on to that knowledge even in some of the toughest times that I've faced, because I know that not everybody is so lucky as to be able to do so. In truth, I can't imagine what it would be like to face the reality of mental illness without my faith in a wounded and risen Christ.

I am not suggesting that illness or suffering of any kind are of themselves good things. I don't think that God wills it that some people should suffer. It may well be true that, for the Christian, "suffering produces endurance, and endurance produces character, and character produces hope" (Romans 5:3–4), but I think that is a reflection on the inevitability of suffering in a fallen creation. When God makes all things new, there will be no more crying or pain or even death (Revelation 21:4). Rather, I think the wounds of Christ are a demonstration that illness or suffering do not separate us from God. In Christ, God knows what it is to suffer.

I also don't want to suggest that any illness, injury or suffering we might face will necessarily be eternal as Christ's is. I believe that privilege and burden is his alone to bear, since he is God incarnate and we are not. Personally, if by grace I am to spend eternity in the joy of God's presence, I certainly do not want to do so in the company of mental illness. That is not to say that in the new creation we will all be forced into some identikit typological ideal of a body (or indeed a mind). I know that for some people who are viewed by the world as 'disabled', their lack of a limb or use of a wheelchair (for example) are just something which makes them who they are much as their hair color or eye color does. I see no reason to think anything other than that continuing to be the case in the resurrection body. Others, though, long not to need a wheelchair, and I believe that too will be the case in the hereafter. It is not an "either/or" binary. It will be rather more subtle. That which needs to be healed will be healed—and that will vary for each person. Christ's wounds are eternal because his saving power is eternal; that does not apply to anyone else.

This side of eternity, however, we must carry our suffering with us. That means we have to allow for it in ourselves and in each other. I think that is a little more tricky with mental illness than it is with physical illness. The wheelchair user knows they need a ramp; the diabetic knows they need insulin. As a society I think we are getting better at making the necessary adjustments for physical challenges, though there is evidently still a lot more to be done. My experience of mental illness is that I often don't know what I need to feel better. In the depths of crisis that doesn't really matter—as I have reflected earlier, at my most unwell I don't think I even knew that I was ill. The self-awareness comes later, and it is very frustrating to know that you are unwell but to have no idea what will improve the situation. And if I don't know myself what I need, I certainly can't explain it to anyone else. There will, however, come times when I *can* articulate at least some of what would be helpful. I think we are collectively a very long way from even recognizing most of the adjustments that would be necessary, let alone putting them into place.

I believe that it is in those moments of helplessness that the suffering Christ is most near to us. In triumphantly carrying those dear tokens of his passion beyond the cross and the tomb, he assures us that our present situation, however confusing or hopeless it may seem, is not the end of the story. All of us also carry with us our own scars, though probably less willingly than Christ carries his. Mine happen largely to be related to mental health. His wounds teach us that our wounds can also be borne, for by him they are borne into the Godhead. I believe that to be true for each of us as individuals. I also believe that is collectively true, that the collective scars caused by societal evils can also be collectively borne because of the joint assurances that God is with us in suffering, and that the wounds are not the end of the story.

All of that is, I think, true. But it can only become a reality for us if we recognize God in our midst; and however much we might wish it, God does not come to us with some perfect easy solution. Rather, we will know God precisely because of his wounds. We may look at his hands and feet and see from those wounds that God is one who is with us in our suffering, yet also promises that our suffering need not define us. The Christian faith is not escapism. It is the promise that God is always with us no matter how bad things get, and the eternal offering of salvation for all through the cross which leads to new life.

The thief of joy

When Peter saw him, he said to Jesus, "Lord, what about him?" Jesus said to him, "If it is my will that he remain until I come, what is that to you? Follow me!"
—John 21:21–22

"WHAT IS THAT TO you?" Jesus poses a question which is a forceful reminder that other people's lives are not ours to lead. That applies equally in the bad times as well as the good. Just as there is little to be gained by being jealous of the good fortune or success of others, there is also little to be gained by wallowing in another's misery or pain. Christ calls us only to take up our own crosses.

I am not suggesting a kind of aloof detachment. As John Donne put it, no man is an island. As Christians, we are bound together as one body of Christ, and the suffering of one is the suffering of all. But there is a difference between the necessary and Christian qualities of empathy and sympathy, and of being utterly consumed by the emotions and achievements (be they positive or negative) of another person. Just as the eye cannot say to the hand, "I have no need of you" (1 Corinthians 12:21), neither can the eye say, "I will become you and take everything of you onto myself". Peter will have plenty of his own opportunities and challenges in the days which lie ahead. The fate of the beloved disciple is not his concern, whether it is a joyful fate or a despairing one. It is easy to spend our time asking, "what about him?" Our Lord's answer to that is, "What is that to you?"

That temptation to compare ourselves to others is not uncommon during recovery from any illness, including mental illness. I tended to do it quite negatively, wondering why I was not recovering as well or as quickly as I imagined other people were. I suppose the opposite must also be true, and that some people enjoy the *schadenfreude* of being better off than others, though that has never been my experience. Either way, I don't think such comparisons are helpful. They certainly don't help me. Each of us can only recover in our own way and in our own time.

There is also another kind of comparison with others of which I think we need to be wary. It isn't *schadenfreude*, because there is no joy in it; it is seeing others who are worse off than yourself, and concluding that their reality somehow negates your own experiences. Quite often I have found myself thinking that my own illness is somehow not valid because I have made some recovery from it, or because it was not so severe as other cases. It becomes a vicious circle—if I do show signs and symptoms of mental illness then I chastise myself for being weak, and if I don't show them then I criticize myself for having given in to them in the past. The fact that both of those responses are negative ones only serves to reinforce the problem. It breeds a kind of health-based Pelagianism, the idea that mental illness can be prevented and defeated by sheer force of individual will. Though wanting to be well naturally plays a part in any recovery, anybody who has experienced mental illness will tell you that it is not that simple.

Comparison with the real or imagined experiences of other people does little to aid recovery. It truly is the thief of joy, because not only does it further darken the days when I am struggling, but it also robs some of the lightness from the days when all seems to be going well. Of course, it is very easy to say that we should not compare ourselves with others. I know first-hand how much more difficult it is to put into practice.

Neither should we compare ourselves too rigorously with ourselves. I've already written here about the problems of comparison with how you were before an experience of mental illness (particularly an acute one). I think the same holds true on much smaller timescales. Whether I had a good or a bad day yesterday does not automatically mean that today will be the same. Recovery from mental illness is not a linear process. Not every step is forward. There are sidesteps, backward steps, steps in the wrong direction. There are giant strides and clumsy stumblings. It is allowable and normal to have good days and bad days, and the one does not make the other somehow invalid. That is just how things are, and that is okay.

But what about him or her? My illness and my recovery are my own, but that does not mean I can do it on my own. Peter and the beloved disciple cannot live each other's lives, but neither can they deny that they are bound together by what they have experienced with Jesus and what they believe. The line between helpful learning and harmful comparison, between much-needed emotional support and dangerous dependence, is a thin and very blurry one. What is right in one situation or for one person may not be right in other circumstances. Here, as much as anywhere else in our experiences, there will be missteps and mistakes. Once we have made mistakes in this area, there is a temptation to withdraw well away from that line and retreat into self-containment. I know that to be true, because I know that I have a tendency to do it myself. It works for a while, sometimes for quite a long while. But it will not work forever. It probably feels "safe", but it promotes stasis rather than the change necessary to recovery.

I think we also sometimes need examples to spur us on—to encourage us that if he or she can get better, so can I. That is fine in itself, but we need to be attentive to what version of another person's story we are hearing. People can make things look better than they actually are. I don't mean that people are necessarily lying (on the whole I think they are probably not), but they will probably not be saying everything. I know I don't say everything, and as I'll reflect later I think that's actually a good thing. But it is worth bearing that in mind when looking at someone else for inspiration. Social media, in particular, usually reflects the edited highlights of a life, limited to the things the user feels comfortable making public. That's how I use mine, and how I read those of other people. Rarely are you getting the whole story—not because I am intending to deceive, but because there are some things that I don't feel the need to broadcast to the world.

Ultimately, none of us can live this life completely alone, whatever our experiences of mental health might be. Nor can we healthily live life in the constant worry of comparison with other people. Thankfully for Peter and for us, Jesus's words do not end there. There is an invitation, perhaps even an instruction. "Follow me!"

While it can be very unhelpful to constantly compare ourselves to other people, I have also found that any sort of recovery from mental illness is impossible in a vacuum. Rebuilding a life may be a process of trial and error, but it helps enormously to have an idea of what you want that life to look like. I think something similar is true of Christian discipleship. It is certainly true where discipleship and mental health interact.

Christ's call to "follow me" is not an invitation to one specific way of being. Peter and the beloved disciple are both called to follow Christ, but it should make no difference to Peter how that calling works out for anyone else. So it is for us—and I have found that trying to be a good disciple of Christ has been a positive influence on my mental health recovery overall. It has not given me a set of pre-determined rules to follow. It does not offer a "tick-box" list of things to guarantee that I will get better. That is not how Christian faith works. What it has given me is the aim of a pattern of living, a twin goal both to make a life which faithfully serves God and also to live one which rejoices in his offer of abundancy.

I am instinctively a little wary of the idea that "God has a plan for each of us". I think it tends to strip us of our God-given free will, and I think it risks making us indifferent to the evils of this world as well as dismissive of the good. I don't think any life runs on pre-determined tracks. I certainly don't think my acute mental health crisis was part of God's plan. What I do think is that when we choose to be attentive to God and to co-operate with him, there is nothing which cannot be worked for some kind of good. I know that the life I am building for myself now is better than that which I had before. It is not easy, and it is taking a lot more time than I originally thought. But it is worth it, and it will be worth it, and I believe it will be more like the life which God wants me to lead. I won't get there by comparing myself now to how I have been in the past. I won't get there by comparing myself to anyone else. Nor will I get there on my own. Whenever I am tempted to ask, "Lord, what about him?" (and that temptation happens very often), I need to remember Our Lord's response, "what is that to you?"—and then I need to remember that too much comparison will get me nowhere. I am only called to live my own life and carry my own cross. I can only be my own part of the body. Christ's instruction is simple: "Follow me".

Speaking out

"You are witnesses of these things."—Luke 24:48

I DO NOT FEEL PARTICULARLY brave for writing this series of short reflections. That fact in itself is a sign that speaking out about mental health and illness is not the taboo it once was, and that must be a good thing. I know that I am not alone in what I have been through and what I live with. If this small volume has helped you to feel the same way, then I am content that it has fulfilled its purpose.

However, I think that speaking out has its time and place. There is also a time to stay silent. A constant pretense that you are okay when you are not helps nobody, least of all you. But in my experience, creating a constant narrative of suffering and pain is also unhelpful. I find that some days, perhaps most days, the thing which I can do best to help myself is just to get on with life even when I don't particularly feel like it. One thing I have learned from my acute mental health crisis is to be better at being honest about when things are really getting on top of me, but I don't see the need or the benefit of maintaining a constant running commentary on whether I am having a good day or a bad day. Many of the bad days have been made more bearable by actually doing things, if only because I can look back at the end of the day and think "at least I achieved something"—even if that something is only going for a run or putting the dishwasher on. It's still better than giving up and staying in bed.

In fact, I think a running commentary of our experiences of mental illness can do more harm than good, because it runs the risk of desensitizing those around us to the extent that when we are truly desperate for help, they are less likely to listen. It is not exactly "the boy who cried wolf", since we are not pretending that we are ill—but if (for example) I complain every day about how tough it is to go to work, even when I am actually managing to do so, I can hardly be surprised if people are less ready to listen, sympathize, and accommodate when I am having a day bad enough that I genuinely can't cope. There is a danger that genuine, even urgent cries for help can become lost in a cacophony of attention-seeking noise. Nobody should feel the need to suffer in silence; but I do think that we have a responsibility to ourselves and to each other to ensure that our speaking out is intended to make a difference, rather than simply to make a noise.

Social media seems to make the latter particularly tempting. It is great for connecting with people, and when I was more ill it was a good way of telling a lot of people at once how I was doing without the strain of having to have dozens if not hundreds of conversations about it; but I do worry that some people seem to play out every detail and nuance of their experience on social media. My instinct is that this in turn encourages people (perhaps especially those with large numbers of followers) to pathologize the everyday vicissitudes of emotion into the language of mental illness in the hope and expectation that it will gain a reaction, which of course it usually does. Dressing up any kind of sadness or challenge as a mental health issue doesn't "raise awareness". If anything, it risks doing the opposite. When we use the language of mental illness in respect of ordinary and expected emotions, we end up without a way of speaking of genuine illnesses.

At its best, the act of witnessing is both timely and perceptive. I feel that the "running commentary" style of speaking out is not timely, because it too easily drowns perceptive moments in an unending sea of noise. The pathologizing of normal human experiences lacks perception in its confusion of healthy emotional responses with unhealthy mental conditions. My hope is that, having successfully broken the taboo surrounding speaking of mental health at all, we may learn to speak about it in a more timely and perceptive manner. At the moment, I worry that we generate a lot of heat and not much light—that the quantity of our speaking is not helping to increase our understanding.

It is that timely and perceptive witness to which Jesus called his followers. Those who heard him directly seem to have understood. Considering how important Jesus was to the authors, the four gospels are remarkably brief works. Only the few days from Maundy Thursday to Easter Day are covered in any real detail. Yet the depth of understanding which they convey, both individually and collectively, has sustained the faith and life of many millions of people. Those first acts of witness by those who had followed Jesus to the cross and then from the empty tomb have inspired countless billions more acts of witness across the world and down the centuries—mostly small, but all with their own significance. At their best, those acts have also been timely and perceptive.

Christ's call to his followers to be witnesses is as relevant today as it was when he first made it, and though the media may have changed, the qualities of effective witness have not. Above all, the call to be a witness is the call to attempt to make a positive difference. That is the call which all the best Christian witnesses down the ages have, in their own way, tried to answer. I suggest that it is a call which we also need to answer both individually and collectively in respect of mental health and illness.

We all need people with whom we can simply "be" in the changes and chances of everyday life. When it comes to "being" with mental illness, we may well be able to rely on family members or close friends. In many cases (certainly in my own), any number of talking therapies such as counselling or psychotherapy may also prove beneficial. Whoever it is, it obviously needs to be somebody we trust, a person with whom we can be completely open and vulnerable. But all that is in private. In public—and this very much includes social media—I think we all need to be far more intentional about trying to make a positive difference when we speak of mental health. I certainly don't mean that we should pretend that a situation or a person (including ourselves) is a positive one when it isn't; there is real and helpful value in honesty about difficult subjects and dark days. What I mean is that our public discussion should be impactful. What we say or write or do should be intended to make a difference, however small that might be.

I believe that Jesus called his followers to impactful witness, and that he still calls us to that same duty and joy to make a difference to the lives of others. Sometimes that will mean talking more about Christianity, but often it means speaking better of it, by which I mean speaking in a way that will actually make a difference to people, and hopefully lead them deeper into faith in God. We can do something similar with mental health. The taboo, at least in Western culture, has been broken. Lots of people now talk about mental illness. But we often still do so too vaguely or abstractly. As I reflected earlier, I didn't think that people weren't talking about my mental illness; I feared and assumed that they were. But almost nobody was talking to me, or giving me the space and security to talk about myself.

That's why we need to speak better of mental health, not more. We all need to work to create a culture in which people can speak properly and honestly of their own experiences in their own time, so that all of us have a better understanding of mental health and the genuine illnesses which can arise in any of us from time to time. We need to be witnesses to the truth, and be prepared to listen to other witnesses to the truth; and we need to be ready and prepared to deal with the consequences of that truth. We need to make our societies so much better than they are so that mental illness can be, if not prevented, at least less aggravated by the pressures of modern life. We need to speak in public with the intention of making a positive difference, rather than just a noise. That is true of so many topics. I am certain that it is true of both Christian faith and mental health. I hope that by sharing some of my own story and thoughts here, I have in my own small way done just that.